Eek!
A Bug

Written by Paul Shipton

Illustrated by Gabriele Antonini

The hamster was asleep.
But a bug was jumping up and down.

The hamster was mad.
He ran after the bug.

He ran near the cat on the stairs.
He trod on the cat's long hair!

The cat ran after the hamster.
The hamster was afraid.

She ran near the dog on the chair.
She hurt the dog's tail!

The dog ran after the cat.
The cat was afraid.

The dog ran near the goat in the flowers. He hit the goat's horn.

The goat ran after the dog.
The dog was afraid.

Then the bug went near the goat.
It did not hurt him.

Eek! It's a bug!

But the goat had never had
such fear!

They all ran.
The goat ran back to the flowers.

The dog ran back to the chair.

The cat ran back to the stairs.

The hamster went back to sleep.

But the bug was jumping up and down.